HAPPINESS

Do you want to be truly happy?

J C RYLE

LIGHTLY EDITED & UPDATED BY MARY DAVIS

EP BOOKS

EP BOOKS

1st Floor Venture House, 6 Silver Court, Watchmead,
Welwyn Garden City, UK, AL7 1TS

www.epbooks.org
admin@epbooks.org

EP Books are distributed in the USA by:
JPL Distribution, 3741 Linden Avenue Southeast, Grand Rapids, MI 49548

orders@jplbooks.com
www.jplbooks.com

British Library Cataloguing in Publication Data available
ISBN 978-1-78397-219-7

CONTENTS

HAPPINESS

'Blessed are the people whose God is the Lord!'
Psalm 144:15

An atheist was once addressing a crowd of people in the open air. He was trying to persuade them that there was no God and no devil, no heaven and no hell, no resurrection, no judgment and no life to come. He advised them to throw away their Bibles and not to mind what preachers said. He recommended them to think as he did and to be like him. He talked boldly. The crowd listened eagerly. It was 'the blind leading the blind.' And both were falling into the ditch.[1]

In the middle of his speech, a poor old woman suddenly pushed her way through the crowd to the place where he was standing. She stood before him. She looked him fully in the face.

---
1   Matthew 15:14 (KJV)

'Sir,' she said, in a loud voice, 'Are you happy?' The atheist looked scornfully at her and gave her no answer. 'Sir,' she said again, 'I ask you to answer my question. Are you happy? You want us to throw away our Bibles. You tell us not to believe what preachers say about the gospel. You advise us to think as you do and be like you. Now before we take your advice, we have a right to know what good we shall get by it. Do your fine new ideas give you much comfort? Do you yourself really feel happy?'

The atheist stopped and he attempted to answer the old woman's question. He stammered and shuffled and fidgeted and endeavoured to explain his meaning. He tried hard to turn the subject. He said, he 'had not come there to preach about happiness.' But it was no use. The old woman stuck to her point. She insisted on her question being answered and the crowd took her side. She pressed him hard with her question and would take no excuse. And at last the atheist was obliged to abandon his speech and sneak off in confusion. He could not reply to the question. His conscience would not let him; he did not dare say that he was happy.

The old woman showed great wisdom in asking the question that she did. The argument she used may seem very simple, but it is actually one of the most powerful that can be used. It is a weapon that has more effect on people's minds than the most elaborate reasoning of the finest brains. Whenever someone begins to take up new views about faith and pretends to despise old biblical Christianity, try driving home at their conscience with the old woman's question. Ask them whether their new views make them feel comfortable within. Ask them whether they can say, with honesty and sincerity, that they are happy. The grand test of a person's faith and religion is this: does it make them happy?

Let me now affectionately invite every reader to consider the subject of this short book. Let me warn you to remember that the salvation of your soul, and nothing less, is closely bound up with the subject. The heart which knows nothing of happiness cannot be right in the sight of God. The soul of a man or woman who feels no peace within cannot be safe.

I intend to explore three points in order to address the subject of happiness. I ask you to pay special attention to each one of them. And I pray that the Spirit of God will write it all on the hearts of everyone who reads this book. First, let me point out some things which are absolutely essential to happiness. Secondly, let me expose some common mistakes about the way to be happy. Thirdly, let me show the way to be truly happy.

I. ABSOLUTE ESSENTIALS TO TRUE HAPPINESS

First of all, I have to point out some things which are absolutely essential to true happiness. Happiness is what everyone longs to obtain. The desire for it is deeply planted in the human heart. Everyone naturally dislikes pain, sorrow and discomfort. Everyone naturally likes ease, comfort and gladness. Everyone naturally hungers and thirsts after happiness. Just as the sick person longs for health and the prisoner of war longs for liberty; just as the dehydrated traveller in a hot country longs to see a cooling fountain, or the ice-bound polar voyager longs to see the sun rising above the horizon—in just the same way, we mere mortals long to be happy. But, sadly, how few of us consider what we really mean when we talk of happiness! Most people's ideas on the subject are vague and indistinct and undefined! They think some people are happy when they are actually miserable; they think others are gloomy and sad when they are truly happy. They day-dream of a happiness which would, in truth, never satisfy their true needs. Let me try to throw a little light on the subject.

WHAT HAPPINESS IS NOT…

True happiness *is not perfect freedom from sorrow and discomfort*— let that never be forgotten. If it were so, there would be no such thing as happiness in the world. Happiness like that is for angels who have never fallen, not for mere mortals. I am talking about the kind of happiness which a sinful, dying, mortal being may confidently expect to achieve. Our whole nature is defiled by sin. Evil abounds in the world. Sickness and death and change are doing their sad work on every front each day. With the world in this state, the highest happiness someone can expect to achieve on earth must necessarily be a mixed thing. If we expect to find any absolutely perfect happiness on this side of the grave, we are expecting what we shall not find.

True happiness *does not consist in laughter and smiles.* The face is very often a poor index of the inward person. There are thousands who laugh loudly and are as 'merry as a grasshopper' in the company of others, but are wretched and miserable in private and almost afraid to be alone. On the other hand, there are hundreds who are grave and serious in their manner, whose hearts are full of solid peace. As one of our own poets has rightly told us, smiles are not worth much: 'one may smile, and smile, and be a villain.'[2]

---

2   William Shakespeare, *Hamlet*, Act 1, Scene 5.

And the eternal word of God teaches us that 'Even in laughter the heart may ache.'[3] Do not talk to me simply about smiling and laughing faces. I want to hear about something more than that when I ask whether someone is happy. A truly happy person will undoubtedly often show their happiness in their face; but someone may have a very merry face, and yet not be happy at all.

Of all deceptive things on earth, nothing is so deceptive as *mere worldly enjoyment and amusement.* It is a hollow empty show, utterly devoid of substance and reality. Listen to the most brilliant public speaker and notice the applause which they receive from an admiring crowd; then follow them to their own private room and you will very likely find them plunged in melancholy despondency. Colonel James Gardiner, who was outwardly cheerful and carefree, confessed that even when he was thought to be most happy, he often wished he was a dog. Look at the smiling beauty in the ballroom and you might suppose that she did not know what it was to be unhappy; but see her the next day in her own home and you may well find her out of sorts with herself and everybody else besides.

Oh, no: worldly enjoyment is not real happiness! There is a certain pleasure about it, I do not deny. There is an animal excitement about it, I do no question that. There is a temporary elevation of spirits about it, I freely accept. But do not call it by the cherished name of 'happiness.' The most beautiful cut flowers stuck into the ground do not make a garden. Not until glass becomes a genuine diamond, or tinsel becomes genuine gold—not

---

3   Proverbs 14:13

until then, do people who laugh and make merry deserve to be called 'happy.'[4]

OUR HIGHEST NEEDS MUST
BE MET AND SATISFIED

To be truly happy, a person's highest needs must be met and satisfied. The requirements of our wondrously created constitution must all be met. There must be nothing about us that cries, 'Give, give,'—and does so in vain, getting no answer. The horse and the ox are happy so long as they are warmed and filled. And why? Because they are satisfied. The little child looks happy when it is clothed, fed and well and in its mother's arms. And why? Because he or she is satisfied. And just so it is with us. Our highest needs must be met and satisfied before we can be truly happy. Every part of us must be filled up. There must be no void, no empty places, no unsupplied cravings. Until then, a person is never truly happy.

And what are our principal needs? Are we just a body? No—we have something more! Each of us has a soul. Are we just our

---

4   Miguel de Cervantes, author of *Don Quixote*, was overwhelmed with a deep cloud of melancholy at a time when all Spain was laughing at his humorous work. Molière, one of the great French comic writers, carried a sadness into his home life which the significant worldly prosperity could never dispel. Samuel Foote, the noted wit of the 18th century, died of a broken heart. Theodore Hooke, the facetious novel writer, who could set everybody laughing, said of himself in his diary, 'I am suffering under a constant depression of spirits, which no one who sees me in society dreams of.' A woebegone stranger consulted a doctor about his health. The doctor advised him to keep up his spirits by going to hear the great comic actor of the day: 'You should go and hear Matthews. He would make you well.' 'Alas, sir,' was the reply, 'I am Matthews himself!'

senses? Can we do nothing but hear and see and smell and taste and feel? No—each of us has a thinking mind and a conscience! Do we have no consciousness of any world, except the one in which we live and move? Of course we do! There is a still small voice within us which often makes itself heard: 'This life is not all there is! There is an unseen world! There is a life beyond the grave.' Yes, it is true! Each of us is fearfully and wonderfully made. Everyone knows it, everyone feels it, if only they would speak the truth. It is utter nonsense to pretend that food and clothing and earthly things alone can make us happy. There are 'soul-needs.' There are 'conscience-needs.' There can be no true happiness until these needs are satisfied.

WE MUST HAVE SOURCES OF GLADNESS WHICH DO NOT DEPEND ON ANYTHING IN THIS WORLD

To be truly happy, a person must have sources of gladness which do not depend on anything in this world. There is nothing on earth which is not stamped with the mark of instability and un-certainty. All the good things which money can buy are only mo-mentary: they either leave us, or we are obliged to leave them. All the sweetest relationships in life are liable to come to an end; death may come any day and cut them off. The person whose happiness depends entirely on things here below, is like the one who builds their house on sand, or leans their weight on a reed.

Do not claim to be happy if your happiness continually hangs on the uncertainties of earth. Your home may be rich in comforts;

your spouse and your children may be all you could desire; your income may be amply sufficient to meet all your needs. But oh, remember, if you have nothing more than this to look to, remember that you stand on the brink of a precipice! Your rivers of pleasure may dry up any day. Your joy may be deep and earnest but it is fearfully short-lived. It has no root. It is not true happiness.

WE MUST BE ABLE TO LOOK IN EVERY DIRECTION WITHOUT UNCOMFORTABLE FEELINGS

To be truly happy, a person must be able to look in every direction without uncomfortable feelings. They must be able to look back to the past without guilty fears; they must be able to look around themselves without discontent; they must be able to look forward without anxious dread. They must be able to sit down and think calmly about things past, present and things to come, and feel prepared. The person who has a direction that he does not like to contemplate or think about is not really happy.

Do not claim to be happy, if you are unable to look steadily either before or behind you. Your present position may be easy and pleasant. You may find many sources of joy and gladness in your profession, your home, your family and your friends. Your health may be good, your spirits may be cheerful. But stop and think quietly over your past life. Can you reflect calmly on all the sins of omission and commission of years gone by? How will they bear up to God's inspection? How will you answer for them on the last day?

And then look forward and think about the years yet to come. Think of the certain end towards which you are hastening: think of death; think of judgment; think of the hour when you will meet God face-to-face. Are you ready for it? Are you prepared? Can you look forward to these things without alarm? Oh, be very sure if you cannot look comfortably on any time but the present, then your boasted happiness is a poor and unreal thing! It is but a white-washed tomb, clean and beautiful on the outside – but bones and corruption within.[5] It is simply a passing thing that lasts but a day, like Jonah's vine.[6] It is not real happiness.

I ask you to fix in your mind this list of things that are essential to happiness, which I have attempted to set before you. Dismiss from your thoughts the many mistaken ideas which circulate on this subject, like counterfeit money. To be truly happy, the needs of your soul and conscience must be satisfied. To be truly happy, your joy must be founded on something more than this world can give you. To be truly happy, you must be able to look in every direction—above, below, behind, in front—and feel that everything is right. This is real, high quality, genuine happiness. This is the happiness I have in view and that I am urging you to think carefully about.

---

5   Matthew 23:27
6   Jonah 4

2. SOME COMMON MISTAKES ABOUT THE WAY TO BE HAPPY

Next, let me expose some common mistakes about the way to be happy. There are several roads which people think will lead to happiness, and there are thousands and tens of thousands of men and women travelling on each of one of those roads. Some think that if only they could get everything they wanted, then they would be happy. Others think that if they do not succeed, then the fault lies in their lack of opportunity and good luck. And they all seem ignorant of the fact that they are hunting shadows; they are chasing after the wind; they are heading in the wrong direction. They are looking for something which can never be found in the place where they are looking for it.

I will mention by name some of the principal delusions about happiness. I do it in love and friendship and compassion towards people's souls. I believe it to be my public duty to warn people against cheats, tricksters and impostors. Oh, how much trouble and sorrow it might save my readers, if they would only believe what I am going to say!

RANK AND GREATNESS
WILL NOT BRING HAPPINESS

It is an utter mistake to suppose that rank and greatness alone can give happiness. The kings and rulers of this world are not necessarily happy. They have troubles and crosses which no-one else knows about. They see a thousand evils which they are unable to remedy. They are slaves working in golden chains and have less real freedom than any in the world. They have burdens and responsibilities laid upon them which are a daily weight on their hearts. The Roman Emperor Antonine often said that 'the imperial power was an ocean of miseries.' Queen Elizabeth I, when she heard a milk-maid singing, wished that she had been born to a lot like hers. Never did our great poet write a truer word than when he said, 'Uneasy lies the head that wears a crown.'[7]

WEALTH WILL NOT BRING HAPPINESS

It is an utter mistake to suppose that riches alone can give happiness. They can enable a person to command and possess everything, but not inward peace. Riches cannot buy a cheerful spirit and a light heart. There are troubles in the getting of them, troubles in the keeping of them, troubles in the using of them, troubles in the disposing of them, troubles in the gathering of

---

7   William Shakespeare, *Henry IV Part 2*, Act 3, Scene 1.

them, and troubles in the scattering of them. The one who said that 'money' was only another name for 'trouble' was wise indeed; also that the same English letters which spelled 'acres' would also spell 'cares.'

INTELLIGENCE
WILL NOT BRING HAPPINESS

It is an utter mistake to suppose that intelligence and scholarship alone can bring happiness. They may occupy a person's time and attention but they cannot really make them happy. Those who increase knowledge often 'increase sorrow'; the more they learn the more they discover their own ignorance.[8] Earthly things do not have the power to minister to a diseased heart. The heart needs something as well as the head; the conscience needs food as well as the intellect. All the secular knowledge in the world will not give someone joy and gladness when he thinks about sickness, death and the grave. Those who have climbed the highest have often found themselves solitary, dissatisfied and empty of peace. The scholarly John Selden, at the close of his life, confessed that all his intelligence and education did not give him such comfort as these four verses of the apostle Paul:

> *For the grace of God has appeared, bringing salvation for*
> *all people, training us to renounce ungodliness and worldly*
> *passions, and to live self-controlled, upright, and god-*
> *ly lives in the present age, waiting for our blessed hope,*
> *the appearing of the glory of our great God and Saviour*

---

8   Ecclesiastes 1:18

*Jesus Christ, who gave himself for us to redeem us from all
lawlessness and to purify for himself a people for his own
possession who are zealous for good works.*[9]

LEISURE TIME AND IDLENESS
WILL NOT BRING HAPPINESS

It is an utter mistake to suppose that idleness alone can give happiness. The labourer who gets up at five in the morning and goes out to work all day in the cold often thinks, as he walks past the rich man's door, 'What a fine thing it must be to have no work to do.' Poor man! He does not really know what he longs for. The most miserable creature on earth is the man who has nothing to do. Work for the hands or work for the head is absolutely essential to human happiness. Without it, the mind feeds upon itself and the whole inward man becomes diseased. The machinery within continues to work, but without something to work upon, it can wear itself to pieces. There was no idleness in the garden of Eden. Adam and Eve had to 'work (the garden) and keep it.'[10] There will be no idleness in heaven. God's 'servants will worship him.'[11] Be certain that the most idle person is the most truly unhappy person!

---

9   Titus 2:11-14
10   Genesis 2:15
11   Revelation 22:3

PLEASURE-SEEKING
WILL NOT BRING HAPPINESS

It is an utter mistake to suppose that amusement and plea-sure-seeking alone can bring happiness. Of all roads that people can take in order to be happy, this is the one that is most com-pletely wrong. Of all the wearisome, empty, dull and unprofitable ways of spending life, this exceeds them all. To think of a sinful, dying creature with an immortal soul expecting to find happiness in feasting and drinking, in dancing and singing, in clothes and company, in ball-going and card-playing, in races and fairs, in hunting and shooting, in crowds, in laughter, in noise, in music, in wine! Surely it is a sight that is enough to make the devil laugh and the angels weep. Even a child will not play with its toys all day long. But when grown up men and women think that they will find happiness in a constant round of amusement, they sink far below a child.

I point out these common mistakes about the way to be happy. I ask you to take careful note of them. I warn you plainly against these pretended short-cuts to happiness, however persuasive they may be. I tell you that if you imagine any of them can lead you to true peace, then you are entirely deceived. Your conscience will never feel satisfied; your immortal soul will never feel easy; your whole inward being will feel uncomfortable and out of health. Take any one of these roads—or take all of them—and, if you have nothing else to look to, you will never find happiness. You may travel on and on and on, and the wished-for object will seem as far away at the end of each stage of life as when you started. You are like someone pouring water into a sieve, or putting money into a bag with holes. You might as well try to make an elephant happy by feeding him with a grain of sand a day as try to satisfy that heart of yours with rank, riches, intelligence, idleness or pleasure.

THE WITNESS OF HUMAN LIVES

Do you doubt the truth of all I am saying? I dare say you do. Then let us turn to the Bible, the great book of human experience, and read over a few lines from its solemn pages. You shall also have the testimony of a few competent witnesses on this great subject I am urging you to think about.

A KING

A king shall be our first witness: Solomon, King of Israel. We know that he had power, wisdom and wealth which far exceeded that of any ruler of his time. We know from his own confession that he tried the great experiment of seeing how far the things of this world can make someone happy. We know the result of this curious experiment from Solomon's own writings. He writes it by the inspiration of the Holy Spirit for the benefit of the whole world in the book of Ecclesiastes. This experiment has surely never been conducted under such favourable circumstances as his; the experiment could never have been more likely to succeed. Yet what is Solomon's testimony? You have it in his own melancholy words: 'All is vanity and a striving after wind.'[12]

---

12   Ecclesiastes 1:14

A FAMOUS LADY

A famous French lady is our next witness: Madam de Pompadour. She was the friend and favourite of Louis XV. She had unbounded influence at the Court of France. She lacked nothing that money could buy. Yet what does she say herself?

> *'What a situation is that of the great! They only live in the future, and are only happy in hope. There is no peace in ambition. I am always gloomy, and often unreasonably so. The kindness of the King, the regard of courtiers, the attachment of my servants, and the fidelity of a large number of friends – motives like these, which ought to make me happy, affect me no longer. I have no longer inclinations for all which once pleased me. I have caused my house at Paris to be magnificently furnished; well it pleased me for two days! My residence at Bellevue is charming but I cannot endure it. Kind people relate to me all the news and adventures of Paris; they think I listen but when they are done, I ask them what they said. In a word, I do not live. I am dead before my time. I have no interest in the world. Everything conspires to embitter my life. My life is a continual death.'*[13]

To such testimony I need not add a single word.

13   Catherine Sinclair, *The Kaleidoscope of Anecdotes and Aphorisms* (London: Schulze & Co, 1851), 33.

A WRITER

A famous German writer will be our next witness: Goethe. It is well known that he was almost idolized by many during his life. His works were read and admired by thousands. His name was known and honoured all over the world wherever German was read. And yet the praise of man (of which he reaped such an abundant harvest) was utterly unable to make Goethe happy. 'He confessed, when about eighty years old, that he could not remember being in a really happy state of mind even for a few weeks together.'[14]

A PEER AND A POET

An English peer and poet is our next witness: Lord Byron. If ever there was someone who ought to have been happy according to the standards of the world, Lord Byron was that man. He began life with all the advantages of English rank and position. He had splendid abilities and powers of mind which the world soon discovered and was ready to honour. He had a sufficient financial means to gratify his every wish and never knew anything of real poverty. Humanly speaking, there seemed nothing to prevent him enjoying life and being happy. Yet, it is a notorious fact that Byron was a miserable man. Misery stands out in his poems, misery creeps out of his letters. Weariness, overindulgence, disgust and discontent appear in everything. He is a solemn warning that rank, title and literary fame alone are not sufficient to make someone happy.

---

14   Sinclair, *Anecdotes & Aphorisms*, 280.

A SCIENTIST

A man of science is next: Sir Humphrey Davy. He was eminently successful in the line of life which he chose, and deservedly so. A distinguished philosopher, the inventor of the famous Davy safety-lamp (which preserved so many poor miners from death), a Baron of the United Kingdom and President of the Royal Society; his whole life seemed a continual career of prosperity. If intelligence alone were the road to happiness, this man at least ought to have been happy. Yet what was the true record of Davy's feelings? We have it in his own melancholy journal towards the end of his life. He describes himself in two painful words: 'Very miserable!'

A HEDONIST

A man of wit and pleasure is our next witness: Lord Chesterfield. He shall speak for himself, his own words from one of his letters.

> *'I have seen the silly round of business and pleasure, and am done with it all. I have experienced all the pleasures of the world and consequently know their futility, and do not regret their loss. I appraise them at their real value which in truth is very low; whereas those who have not experience always overrate them. They only see their cheery outside, and are dazzled with their glare; but I have been behind the scenes. I have seen all the coarse pulleys and dirty ropes which exhibit and move the gaudy machine, and I have seen and smelled the candles which illuminate the whole decoration, to the astonishment and admiration of the ignorant audience. When I reflect on what I have seen, what I have heard, and what I have done, I cannot persuade*

myself that all that frivolous hurry of bustle and pleasure of
the world had any reality. I look on all that is past, as one
of those romantic dreams which opium occasions, and I do
by no means wish to repeat the nauseous dose for the sake
of the fleeting dream.'

These sentences speak for themselves. I need not add to them one single word.

POLITICIANS

The statesmen and politicians who have swayed the destinies of the world ought, by rights, to be our last witnesses. But, in the spirit of Christian charity, I will resist naming them. It makes my heart ache when I run my eye over the list of famous names from English history and think how many have worn out their lives in a breathless struggle for position and distinction. How many of our greatest men and women have died of broken hearts, disappointed, disgusted and worn out with constant failure! Many have left on record some humbling confession that, in the height of their powers, they were pining for rest, as a caged eagle yearns for freedom! Many whom the world congratulates for being in complete control are, in fact, little better than slaves, chained and unable to get free! I am sorry to say that there are many sad examples, both among the living and the dead, that to be great and powerful is not necessarily the same thing as being happy.

I think it is very likely that some people will not believe what I am saying. I know how deceitful the heart can be when it comes to the subject of happiness. People are unusually reluctant to believe the truths that I am proposing about the way to be happy. Please bear with me while I say something more.

THE RICH AND FAMOUS

Come and stand with me some afternoon in the heart of the City of London. Let us watch the faces of most of the wealthy people that we see leaving their offices at the end of the day. Some of them are worth hundreds of thousands of pounds, some of them are worth millions. But what is written in the faces of these serious men and women that we see swarming out from Lombard Street and Cornhill, from the Bank of England and the Stock Exchange? What do those deep lines which furrow so many a forehead mean? What about that air of anxious thoughtfulness which is worn by five out of every six people we meet? These things tell a serious tale. They tell us that it needs something more than gold and bank notes to make people happy.

Come next and stand with me near the Houses of Parliament, in the middle of a busy session. Let us scan the faces of nobles whose names are familiar and well-known all over the civilized world. There you may see, on some fine May evening, the mightiest statesmen and women in England hurrying to a debate, like eagles to the carcass. Each has the power of good or evil in their tongue, which is a fearful thing to contemplate. Each may say things before tomorrow's sun dawns which may affect the peace and prosperity of nations and shake the world. There you may see the men and women who hold the reins of power and government already; there you may see men and women who are watching every day for an opportunity of snatching those reins out of their hands and governing instead of them. But what do their faces tell us as they rush to their posts? What may be learned from their care-worn expressions? What may be read from their wrinkled foreheads, so absent-looking and sunk in thought? They teach us a solemn lesson. They teach us that it needs something more than political greatness to make us happy.

Come next and stand with me in the most fashionable part of London, in the height of the season. Let us visit Regent Street or Pall Mall, Hyde Park or Mayfair. How many attractive faces and splendid carriages we shall see! How many people we can count up in just an hour who seem to have the best of everything: beauty, wealth, rank, fashion and crowds of friends! But, sadly, how few we shall see who appear happy! In how many faces we shall see weariness, dissatisfaction, discontent, sorrow or unhappiness, as clearly as if it were written with a pen? Yes, it is a humbling lesson to learn, but a very wholesome one. It needs something more than rank and fashion and beauty to make people happy.

COUNTRY-DWELLERS

Come next and walk with me through some quiet country village in rural England. Let us visit some secluded corner in our beautiful countryside, far away from great towns and fashionable entertainment and political strife. There are plenty such places to be found: rural villages where there are no street lamps, public houses or beer shops; where there is work for all the workers, and a church for all the population, and a school for all the children, and a minister of the gospel to look after the people. You would surely think that we would find happiness here! Surely places like these must be a very haven of peace and joy!

Go into the quiet-looking cottages, one by one, and you will soon realize the truth. Discover the inner history of each family and you will soon change your mind. You will soon discover that backbiting and lying and slandering and envy and jealousy and pride and laziness and drinking and extravagance and lust and petty quarrels can murder happiness in the country, quite as much as in the town! No doubt a rural village sounds pretty in poetry and looks beautiful in pictures; but, in sober reality, human nature is the same evil thing everywhere. Unfortunately, it takes something more than a home in a quiet country village to make any child of Adam a happy man or woman!

BE WISE

I know these are age-old thoughts. They have been said a thousand times before without effect and I suppose they will be said without again effect. The stubbornness with which we seek happiness where happiness cannot be found is extraordinary. There is no greater proof of the corruption of human nature than this. Century after century, wise men and women have left a record of their experience about the way to be happy. Century after century, people insist that they know the way perfectly well themselves and need no advice from others. They cast the warnings to the winds; and each one rushes to walk on their own favourite path. As Psalm 39 says, they walk about as a shadow, they are in turmoil for nothing.[15] They wake up when it is too late to find that their

---

15   Psalm 39:6

whole life has been a great mistake. Their eyes are blinded and they cannot see that their dreams are as flimsy and fruitless as the mirage in the African desert. Like the tired traveller in those deserts, they think they are approaching a lake of cooling waters; like the same traveller, they find to their dismay that this imagined lake was a dazzling optical delusion and that they are still helpless in the midst of burning sands.

Are you a young person? I beg you to accept the affectionate warning of a minister of the gospel and not to look for happiness where happiness cannot be found. Do not look for it in riches; do not look for it in power and rank; do not look for it in pleasure; do not look for it in intelligence. They are all bright and dazzling fountains and their waters taste sweet. A crowd is standing round and will not leave them; but please remember that God has written over each of these fountains, 'Everyone who drinks of this water will be thirsty again.'[16] Remember this and be wise.

Are you poor? Are you tempted to think that if you had the rich person's place, that you would be quite happy? Resist the temptation and cast it behind you. Do not envy your wealthy neighbours; be content with the things that you have. Happiness does not depend on houses or possessions. Silks and satins cannot shut out sorrow from the heart. Castles and fine halls cannot prevent anxiety and trouble coming in at their doors. There is as much misery riding and driving about in splendid carriages as there is walking about on foot. There is as much unhappiness in large mansions as there is in poor cottages. Please remember the common mistakes people make about happiness, and be wise!

---

16   John 4:13

3. THE WAY TO BE REALLY HAPPY

L et me now, lastly, point out the way to be really happy. There is a clear-cut path which leads to happiness, if only we would take it. There has never been a person who travelled on that path and failed to achieve his goal.

It is a path which is open to all. It needs neither wealth, nor rank, nor intelligence in order to walk on it. It is for the servant as well as for the master; it is for the poor as well as for the rich. No-one is excluded, except those who exclude themselves.

It is the one and only path. Everyone who has ever been happy since the days of Adam has journeyed on it. There is no 'royal road' to happiness. If kings want to be happy, they must be content to go side by side with the lowliest of their subjects.

BE A REAL, THOROUGH-GOING, TRUE-HEARTED CHRISTIAN

Where is this path? Where is this road? I will tell you.

The way to be happy is to be a real, thorough-going, true-hearted Christian. The Bible declares it, and experience proves it. The true Christian, the believer in Christ, the child of God—they, and they alone, are the happy ones.

It sounds too simple to be true; it seems at first sight so plain a recipe that it is not to be believed. But the greatest truths are often the simplest. The secret which many of the wisest people on earth have utterly failed to discover is revealed to the humblest believer in Christ. I repeat it deliberately and I challenge the world to disprove it: the true Christian is the only truly happy person.

What do I mean when I speak of a *true* Christian? Do I mean everybody who goes to church or chapel? Do I mean everybody who professes an orthodox creed and bows his head at the belief? Do I mean everybody who professes to love the gospel? No, indeed! I mean something very different. Not everyone who is called a Christian is a Christian. I am talking about the one who is a Christian in heart and life; the one who has been taught by the Holy Spirit to feel his sins deeply; the one who really rests all their hopes on the Lord Jesus Christ and his atonement; the one who has been born again and really lives a spiritual, holy life; the one whose faith is not a mere Sunday coat but a compelling principle governing every day of their life. This is what I mean when I speak of a true Christian.

What do I mean when I say the true Christian is *happy*? Do they have no doubts or fears? No anxieties or troubles? No sorrows or cares? Does he or she never feel pain or shed any tears? Far be it from me to say anything of the kind. The true Christian has a weak body and is frail like any other; they have feelings and passions like everyone born into this world; they live in a changing society. But deep down in their heart, they have a mine of solid peace and substantial joy which is never exhausted. This is true happiness.

Do I say that all true Christians are *equally* happy? No, not for a moment! There are babies in Christ's family as well as old men and women; there are weak members of the spiritual body as well as strong ones; there are delicate lambs as well as sheep; there are towering cedars of Lebanon as well as spindly hyssop growing on the wall. There are degrees of grace and degrees of faith. Those who have most faith and grace will have most happiness. But all of them, generally speaking, are happy when compared with the people of the world.

Do I say that all true Christians are equally happy *at all times*? No, not for a moment! All have their ebbs and flows of comfort: some, like the Mediterranean Sea, almost imperceptibly; some, like the massive tides at Chepstow, 50 or 60 feet at a time. Their bodily health is not always the same; their earthly circumstances are not always the same; those they love will sometimes bring them great anxiety; they themselves are sometimes overtaken by faults and weaknesses, and they walk in darkness. They sometimes give way to inconsistencies and persistent sins, and lose their sense of forgiveness. But, as a general rule, the true Christian has a deep pool of peace within them which, even at the lowest, is never entirely dry. I use the words, 'as a general rule' advisedly. When a believer falls into such a horrible sin as, say, that of David, it would be monstrous to talk of his feeling inward peace.[17]

THE TRUE CHRISTIAN'S CONSCIENCE IS AT PEACE

The true Christian is the only truly happy person because their conscience is at peace. The Christian's conscience—that mysterious witness for God which is so mercifully placed within us—is fully satisfied and at rest. It recognizes that the death of Christ completely cleanses away all its guilt. It recognizes that the priesthood and mediation of Christ is a complete answer to all its fears. It recognizes that, through the sacrifice and death of Christ, God can now be *just*—and yet, at the same time, be the *justifier* of the ungodly. Conscience no longer bites and stings and makes its possessor afraid of himself or herself. The Lord Jesus Christ has amply met all its requirements. Conscience is no longer the enemy of the true Christian, but their friend and adviser. Therefore, the true Christian is happy.

THE TRUE CHRISTIAN KNOWS THAT ALL IS WELL WITH HIS SOUL

The true Christian is the only truly happy person because they can sit down quietly and think about their soul. They can look behind

---

17   2 Samuel 11-12

them and in front, they can look within and around and feel, 'All is well.' The true Christian can think calmly about their past life and, however many and great sins they remember, they can take comfort in the knowledge that they are all forgiven. The righteousness of Christ covers all, as Noah's flood covered the highest hills.[18]

The true Christian can think calmly about things to come and not be afraid. Sickness is painful; death is solemn; the judgment day is a solemn thing—but if Christ is for us, who can be against us? We have nothing to fear.[19] The true Christian can think calmly about the holy God whose eyes see all his or her actions and feel: he is my Father, my reconciled Father in Christ Jesus. I am weak; I am unworthy, but, in Christ, he regards me as his dear child and is well pleased. What a privilege it is to be able to think these things and not be afraid! I can completely understand the mournful complaint of the prisoner in solitary confinement. Although he had warmth, food, clothing and work, he was not happy. Why? He said, 'I was obliged to think.'

THE TRUE CHRISTIAN HAS SOURCES OF HAPPINESS INDEPENDENT OF THIS WORLD

The true Christian is the only truly happy person because they have sources of happiness which are entirely independent of this world. They have something which cannot be affected by sickness

18   Genesis 7:20
19   Romans 8:31

or by death, by private losses or by public calamities. They have 'the peace of God, which surpasses all understanding.'[20] They have a hope laid up for them in heaven; a treasure which moth and rust cannot destroy; a house which will never fall down.[21]

A loving wife may die; a heart may be torn in two; the life of a darling child may be taken; we may be left alone in this cold world; earthly plans may be crossed; health may fail, but all this time the true Christian has an inheritance which nothing can harm. We have a friend who never dies, eternal possessions beyond the grave and nothing can deprive us of that. The lower springs of water may fail but the upper springs never run dry. This is real happiness.

THE TRUE CHRISTIAN HAS
THE RIGHT PRIORITIES

The true Christian is happy because their heart, mind and will are in the right place. Their abilities are directed to right ends. Their heart is not set on things below, but on things above. Their will is not dedicated to self-indulgence, but is submissive to the will of God. Their mind is not absorbed in wretched, transient trivialities. They want useful work and they enjoy the luxury of doing good. Who does not know the misery of chaos and disorder? Who has not tasted the discomfort of a house where everything and everybody is in the wrong place? The heart of an unconverted person is like that house. Saving grace puts everything in that heart in

20   Philippians 4:7
21   eg Colossians 1:5; Matthew 6:19-20; Matthew 7:24-27

its right position. The things of the soul come first and the things of the world come second. Anarchy and confusion end; unruly passions no longer run loose. Christ reigns over the whole person and each part of him or her does its appropriate work.

The heart of the Christian is the only heart that is truly in order. The Christian lays aside their pride and self-will; they sit at the feet of Jesus, in their right mind. They love God and other people and so they are happy. In heaven, everyone is happy because they all do God's will perfectly. And the nearer someone gets to this standard, the happier they will be.

THE TRUE CHRISTIAN HAS HAPPINESS IN SPITE OF DIFFICULTY

The plain truth is that without Christ, there is no happiness in this world. Only Christ can give the gift of the eternal Comforter. He is the sun; without him, we never feel warm. He is the light; without him, we are always in the dark. He is the bread; without him, we are always starving. He is the living water; without him, we are always thirsty.

Give someone whatever you think they would like, place them wherever you please, surround them with all the comforts you can imagine, it makes no difference. Separate them from Christ, the Prince of Peace, and that person cannot be happy.

Give someone a share in Christ's inheritance and they will be happy in spite of poverty. They will tell you that they lack nothing that is really good. They are provided for, they have all that they need here and now and they have riches in eternity. They have food to eat which the world knows nothing of. They have friends who never leave them nor forsake them. The Father and the Son come to them, and make their home with them; the Lord Jesus Christ will eat with them, and they will eat with Christ.[22]

Give someone a share in Christ's inheritance and they will be happy in spite of sickness. Their flesh may groan, their body may be worn out with pain, but their heart will rest and be at peace. One of the happiest people I ever saw was a young woman who had been hopelessly ill for many years with disease of the spine. She lay in a poor attic without a fire; the straw thatch was less than two feet above her face, and she had not the slightest hope of recovery. But she was always rejoicing in the Lord Jesus. The spirit triumphed mightily over the flesh. She was happy because Christ was with her.

Give someone a share in Christ's inheritance and they will be happy in spite of countless public calamities. The government of the country may be thrown into confusion; rebellion and disorder may turn everything upside-down; laws may be trampled underfoot; justice and fairness may be infringed; freedom may be thrown to the ground; 'might' may prevail over 'right'—but still their heart will not fail. They will remember that the kingdom of Christ will one day be established. They will say, like the old Scottish minister who was unshaken throughout the turmoil of

---

22   Revelation 3:20

the French revolution: 'It is all right. It shall be well with the righteous!'

OBJECTIONS?

I know that Satan hates the doctrine which I am endeavouring to press upon you. I have no doubt he is filling your mind with objections and arguments, and trying to persuade you that I am wrong. I am not afraid to meet these objections head on. Let us bring them forward and see what they are.

You may tell me that you know many *very religious people* who are not happy at all. You see them attending public worship week by week. You know that they are never missing from church. But you see no sign of the peace which I have been describing in them.

But are you sure that these people you speak of are true believers in Christ? Are you sure that, with all their appearance of faith, they are genuinely born again and converted to trust in God? Is it not very likely that they simply have the *name* of Christianity, without the reality; and a form of godliness, without the power? I am afraid that you have to realize that people may do many religious acts but possess no saving faith! Mere formal, ceremonial Christianity cannot make people happy. We need something more than going to church to give us peace. There must be real, vital union with Christ. It is not the *formal* Christian but the *true* Christian who is happy.

You may tell me that you know *really spiritually-minded and converted people* who do not seem happy. Perhaps you have often heard them complaining about their own hearts and groaning over their own wickedness. They seem to you to be all doubts and anxieties and fears; and you want to know, where is their happiness? Where is that happiness which I have been talking about so much?

I do not deny that there are many believers like the ones you describe, and I am sorry for it. I agree that there are many believers who live far below their privileges and seem to know nothing of joy and peace of believing. But did you ever ask any of these people whether they would give up their Christianity and go back to the world? Did you ever ask them, after all their groans and doubts and fears, whether they think they would be happier if they stopped following Christ? Did you ever ask those questions? I am certain that, if you did, even the weakest and most immature believers would all give you the same answer: I am certain they would tell you that they would rather cling to their little scrap of hope in Christ than possess the world. I am sure they would all answer: 'Our faith is weak, if we have any; our grace is small, if we have any; our joy in Christ is next to nothing at all, but we cannot give up what we have got.' With Job, they would say, 'Though the Lord slays us, we must cling to him.'[23] The root of happiness lies very deep in many a poor, weak believer's heart, where neither leaves nor blossoms are to be seen!

But you will tell me, lastly, that you cannot believe that *most Christians* are happy, because they are so grave and serious. You do not believe that they really possess this happiness I have been de-

---

23   Job 13:15

scribing because their faces do not show it. You doubt the reality of their joy because it is hardly evident.

I might easily repeat what I said at the beginning of this short book: that a happy face is no certain proof of a happy heart. But I will not do so. Rather, I will ask you whether you yourself may not be the cause why believers look grave and serious when you meet them? If you are not a believer yourself, you surely cannot expect them to look at you without some sadness. They see you on the road to destruction and that alone is enough to give them pain. They see thousands like you, hurrying towards weeping and endless woe. Isn't it possible that such a sight each day should cause them grief? Your company, very likely, is one cause why they are serious. Wait until you are a believer yourself before you pass judgment on the seriousness of converted people. See them in groups of people where everyone is of one heart and everyone loves Christ and, so far as my own experience goes, you will find no others so truly happy as true Christians.

When the atheist David Hume asked Bishop George Horne why religious people always looked melancholy, the learned churchman replied, 'The sight of you, Mr Hume, would make any Christian melancholy.'

I repeat my claim; and I repeat it boldly, confidently and de-liberately: I say that there is no happiness among worldly people which can possibly compare with that of the true Christian. All other happiness compared with theirs is moonlight compared with sunshine, brass compared with gold. Boast, if you like, of the laughter and merriment of unbelievers; sneer, if you like, at the gravity and seriousness of many Christians. I have looked this whole subject directly in the face and my mind is unchanged on the matter. I say that the true Christian alone is the one who is truly happy, and the way to be happy is to be a true Christian.

CONCLUSIONS

And now I am going to close this book with a few words of clear application. I have tried to show what is essential to true happiness. I have tried to expose the errors of many views which dominate upon the subject. I have tried to point out in plain and unmistakable words the only way that true happiness can be found. Allow me to conclude with an affectionate appeal to the consciences of everyone who has stumbled across this short book.

A QUESTION: ARE YOU REALLY HAPPY?

First, let me beg every reader to ask themselves this serious question: are you happy? High or low, rich or poor, master or servant, manager or labourer, young or old, this is a question that deserves an answer: are you really happy?

To the successful and sophisticated person who cares for nothing except the things of today, neglecting the Bible, making a god of business or money, providing for everything but the day of judgment, scheming and planning for everything but eternity, I put this question to you: are you happy? You know you are not.

To the foolish person who is trifling away their life in foolish frivolity, spending hour after hour on their mortal body which will soon pass away, making an idol of clothes and fashion and excitement and human praise as if this world was all there was, I put this question to you: are you happy? You know you are not.

To the young person who is intent on pleasure and self-indulgence, fluttering from one idle pastime to another, like a moth around the flame of a candle, imagining themselves clever and well informed, but too wise to be led by pastors and ignorant that they are caught by the devil's snare, like the beast that is led to the slaughter, I put this question to you: are you happy? You know you are not.

Yes, each and every one of you, you are not happy! And in your own conscience, you know it well. You may not admit it, but it is sadly true. There is a great empty place in each of your hearts and nothing will fill it. Pour into it whatever you like—money, education, rank or pleasure—and it will still be empty. There is an aching place in each of your consciences, and nothing will heal it. Unbelief cannot; liberalism cannot; Roman Catholicism cannot—they are all ineffective medicines. Nothing can heal it except the one thing you have not tried: the simple gospel of Christ. Yes, you are indeed a miserable person! Listen to my warning today:

you will never be happy until you are converted to Christ. You could no more expect to feel the sunshine on your face when you turn your back to it, as to feel happy when you turn your back on God and on Christ.

A WARNING: BEWARE LIVING A LIFE WHICH CANNOT MAKE YOU HAPPY

Next, let me warn all who are not true Christians about the foolishness of living a life which cannot make them happy.

I pity you from the bottom of my heart and I long for you to open your eyes and be wise. I stand like a watchman on the look-out tower of the everlasting gospel. I see you sowing seeds of eternal misery for yourselves and I want to call on you to stop and think, before it is too late. I long that God may show you your foolishness. You are digging reservoirs, *leaking* reservoirs, which can hold no water. You are spending your time and strength and emotions on things that will give you no return for all your efforts, spending your money on that which is not bread, and your work on that which does not satisfy.[24] It is as if you are building a tower of Babel of your own design, ignorant of the fact that God will show contempt for all your schemes for achieving happiness, because you attempt to be happy without him.[25]

Wake up from your dreams, I beg you, and show yourselves to be truly wise. Think of the uselessness of living a life of which

---

24   Isaiah 55:2
25   Genesis 11:1-9

you will be ashamed when you die; and of having a mere nominal religion which will utterly fail you when it is most needed.

Open your eyes and look around the world. Tell me who was ever really happy without God and Christ and the Holy Spirit. Look at the road on which you are travelling. See the footsteps of those who have gone before you, see how many have turned away from it and confessed that they were wrong.

I warn you plainly that if you are not a true Christian, you will miss out on happiness in the present world, as well as in the world to come. Please believe me, the way of *happiness* and the way of *salvation* are one and the same! The person who wants things his own way and refuses to serve Christ will never be really happy. But the one who serves Christ has the promise of both lives. They are happy on earth and will be happier still in heaven.

If you are not happy in either this world or the next, I regret to say that it will be all your own fault. Think about it. Do not be guilty of such enormous foolishness. Who does not mourn over the plight of the drunkard, the drug-taker and the suicidal? But there is no foolishness like that of the foolish 'child of the world.'

A PLEA: SEEK HAPPINESS
IN THE ONLY PLACE IT CAN FOUND

Next, let me beg all readers of this book who are not yet happy to seek happiness in the only place it can be found.

The keys of the way to happiness are in the hands of the Lord Jesus Christ. He is appointed and approved by God the Father to give the bread of life to those who hunger and to give the water of life to those who thirst.[26] There is a door which has not—and cannot—be opened by riches or rank or education; but is now ready to open to every humble, praying believer. If you want to be happy, come to Christ! Come to him, confessing that you are weary of your own ways and want rest; that you find you have no power or strength to make yourself holy or happy or fit for heaven; and have no hope, except in him. Tell him this unconditionally. This is coming to Christ.

Come to him, imploring him to show you his mercy and grant you his salvation; imploring him to wash you in his own blood and take your sins away; imploring him to speak peace to your conscience and heal your troubled soul. Tell him all this unconditionally. This is coming to Christ.

You have everything to encourage you. The Lord Jesus himself invites you. He says to you as well as to others, 'Come to me, all who labour and are heavy laden, and I will give you rest. Take my yoke upon you, and learn from me; for I am gentle and lowly in heart, and you will find rest for your souls. For my yoke is easy, and my burden is light.'[27] Wait for nothing. You may feel unworthy. You may feel as if you have not repented enough. But wait no longer. Come to Christ.

---

26   John 6:35
27   Matthew 11:28-30

You have everything to encourage you. Thousands have walked in the way you are invited to enter and have found it good. At one point, like you, they served the world and plunged deeply into foolishness and sin. At one point, like you, they became weary of their wickedness and they longed for deliverance and rest. They heard of Christ and his willingness to help and save; they came to him by faith and prayer, after many doubts and hesitations. They found him to be a thousand times more gracious than they had expected. They relied on him and were happy; they carried his cross and tasted peace. Oh, that you would walk in their steps.

I beg you, by the mercies of God, to come to Christ. In view of the fact that you want to be happy, I beg you to come to Christ. Shake off any delay. Awake from your slumber; get up and be free! Come to Christ today.

SOME ADVICE: HOW TO BECOME EVEN HAPPIER

Lastly, let me offer a few hints to all true Christians who wish to increase and promote their happiness. I offer these hints with hesitation. I want to apply them to my own conscience as well as to yours. You have found serving Christ to be a source of happiness. I have no doubt that you feel such sweetness in Christ's peace that you would gladly know more of it. I am sure that these hints deserve attention.

Believers, if you want to be even happier in Christ's service, work hard each year to *grow in grace*. Beware of standing still. The holiest men are always the happiest. Let your aim be every year to be more holy; to know more, to feel more, to see more of the fullness of Christ. Do not rest upon old grace; do not be content with the degree of grace that you have so far attained.

Search the Scriptures more earnestly; pray more fervently; hate sin more; put an end to self-will more and more; become humbler; seek more direct personal communion with the Lord Jesus; strive to walking daily with God, as Enoch did; keep your conscience clear of little sins; do not grieve the Holy Spirit; avoid arguments and disputes about lesser matters of faith; lay firmer hold upon the great truths without which no-one can be saved. Remember and practise these things and you will be even happier.

Believers, if you want to be even happier in Christ's service, work hard each year to *be more thankful*. Pray that you may know more and more what it is to 'rejoice in the Lord.'[28] Learn to have a deeper sense of your own wretched sinfulness and wickedness; to be more deeply grateful that, by the grace of God, you are what you are. I am afraid that there is too much complaining and too little thanksgiving among the people of God! There is too much grumbling and coveting things that we do not have. There is too little praising and blessing for the many undeserved mercies that we *do* have. Oh, that God would pour out upon us a great spirit of thankfulness and praise!

Believers, if you want to be even happier in Christ's service, work hard each year to *do more good*. Look around at your circumstances—the circle in which your lot is cast—and make yourself

28   Philippians 3:1

available to be useful. Seek to reflect the character of God: he is not only good, but he also *does* good.[29] I am afraid that there is far too much selfishness among believers in the present day! There is far too much lazy, sitting by the fire, nursing our own spiritual diseases and croaking over the state of our own hearts. Get up and be useful in your day and in your generation! Is there no one that you can speak to? Is there no one that you can write to? Is there literally nothing that you can do for the glory of God and the benefit of your fellow human being? There is much that you might do, if you had only the desire. For your own happiness' sake get up and do it, without delay. The bold, outspoken, working Christians are always the happiest. The more you do for God, the more you will find that God will do for you.[30]

The compromising, procrastinating Christian can never expect to taste perfect peace.

The most committed Christian will always be the happiest of people.

'The desire for happiness is deeply planted in the human heart.'

---

29   Ps 119:68
30   eg Hebrews 6:10, John 4:34

This short book was written many years ago, but its message remains as relevant as ever. The author wants each of us to experience true, profound, lasting happiness. He presents his material with his typical gentleness, humility, clarity, encouragement and a striking lack of guilt-trips. Read and be inspired to grow in your relationship with our Lord Jesus Christ.

This edition takes J C Ryle's very beautiful 19th century prose and revises it slightly to make it more accessible to 21st century readers. If you would like to read it in his original words, it is available free online: www.tracts.ukgo.com/ryle_happiness.pdf